— Animal Trackers —
TRACKING ANIMAL
NUMBERS

Tom Jackson

raintree

a Capstone company — publishers for children

Raintree is an imprint of Capstone Global Library Limited, a company incorporated in
England and Wales having its registered office at 7 Pilgrim Street, London EC4V 6LB
Registered company number 6695582

www.raintree.co.uk
myorders@raintree.co.uk

ISBN: 978-1-4747-0234-8

For Brown Bear Books Ltd:
Text: Tom Jackson
Designer: Lynne Lennon
Design Manager: Keith Davis
Editorial Director: Lindsey Lowe
Children's Publisher: Anne O'Daly
Picture Manager: Sophie Mortimer
Production Director: Alastair Gourlay

British Library Cataloguing in Publication Data
A full catalogue record for this book is available from the British Library.

Acknowledgements
t=top, c=centre, b=bottom, l=left, r=right

Front cover: Suzanne Long/Alamy
1, Jeff Rotman/Alamy; 4, Mike Hewitt/Getty Images News/Thinkstock; 5t, Dennis W. Donohue/Shutterstock; 5b, worac_sp/
Shutterstock; 6, David Schrader/iStock Thinkstock; 7, Chunumunu/Istock Editiorial/Thinkstock; 8, Suzanne Long/Alamy; 9t,
Nigel Cattlin/FLPA; 9b, K Adams66/Thinkstock; 10, Blincwinkle/Wothe/Alamy; 11, Gerry Ellis/Monden Pictures/FLPA; 12-13,
Bildagentur Zoonar GmbH/Shutterstock; 13t, NASA; 14, Christian Ziegler/Minden Pictures/FLPA; 15t, Joe Dube/Shutterstock;
15b, Waddell Images/Shutterstock; 16, Purestock/Thinkstock; 17t, Nicola Keegan/Shutterstock; 17b, USGS; 18, Dung Vo Trung/
Corbis; 19, Ondreicka/Dreamstime; 20, Jeff Rotman/Alamy; 21, Sarit Wuttisan/Shutterstock; 22, Christian Ziegler/Minden
Pictures/FLPA; 23, Charles Brutlag/Shutterstock; 24, Images & Stories/Alamy; 25, Aleksandar Milutinovic/Shutterstock; 26c,
Lars S. Madsen/Alamy; 26b, Marek R. Swadzba/Shutterstock; 27, Cyril Ruoso/Minden Pictures/FLPA; 29c, Funky Frog Stock/
Shutterstock; 29b, Jupiter Images/Thinkstock; 30t, Albin Ebert/Shutterstock.

All Artworks © Brown Bear Books Ltd
Brown Bear Books has made every attempt to contact the copyright holder.
If anyone has any information please contact licensing@brownbearbooks.co.uk.

Some words are shown in bold, **like this**. You can find out
what they mean by looking at the glossary.

Printed in China
19 18 17 16 15
10 9 8 7 6 5 4 3 2 1

CONTENTS

WHY WE TRACK ANIMAL NUMBERS

Scientists count animals for two main reasons. They track the number of **endangered** animals so that they can be protected from becoming **extinct**. Researchers also record how many different animals live in an area to understand more about wildlife.

This is a flock of starlings. There are too many to count. Scientists have to guess their number instead.

ANIMAL GROUPS

Scientists often have to count animals that gather in large groups. Some animals stay together for safety. Others do it to make it easier to hunt prey. Counting the animals in these groups is important for working out how animals survive in their different **habitats**.

The snow leopard of Central Asia is endangered. Scientists keep track of its numbers so it does not become **extinct**. There are about 5,000 snow leopards in the wild.

ESTIMATING NUMBERS

The number of animals in an area is called its population. Animal groups can be huge. Some antelope herds can have 250,000 animals. Billions of sardines form a shoal off the coast of South Africa every summer. Scientists cannot count all the animals. They **estimate** the number. This is like guessing. An estimated answer is never exactly right. However, scientists always use the same methods to estimate numbers. This means they can be sure their answers are as near to the real numbers as possible.

This swarm of bees is looking for a new place to live. Scientists have counted 80,000 individual bees in the largest bees' nests. When the nest gets too crowded, a small swarm will leave and build a new one.

COUNTING POPULATIONS

For endangered animals, scientists can sometimes track exact numbers. The Vancouver Island marmot (a ground squirrel) is one of the world's rarest animals. There are only 35 left in the wild. Just one marmot death would cause a major problem. Scientists need to keep track of the populations of endangered **species**.

COUNTING
BY SIGHT

The simplest way of tracking animal numbers is to count animals by sight. However, counting a large group of animals requires a different technique from tracking endangered or **solitary** animals.

These spinner dolphins have gathered in a **superpod** made up of all the dolphins in the area. This is a good opportunity for scientists to count them.

COUNTING GROUPS

In 1849, a South African named John Fraser saw an enormous herd of antelopes in his town. There were so many animals, it took three days for the herd to pass. He couldn't count them. Today, modern scientists would be able to estimate their numbers using a simple method.

Scientists pick a small section of a grazing herd and count all the animals in that area. There may be 50, for example. The size of this area is compared with the rest of the herd that can be seen by the scientists. Let's say the counting area is one-tenth the size of that of the rest of the herd. That means the total number of animals in view is about 10 x 50, or 500.

ANIMAL SURVEY

This technique does not work for rare animals that are hard to find, such as rhinoceroses. Instead, researchers create **surveys**, recording piles of dung, footprints and other signs that show how many individual animals live in the area.

Tourists taking an elephant ride in Nepal are lucky to see this Indian rhino. There are just 378 rhinos left in the country of Nepal.

FACT: In 2014, 35,000 walruses gathered on a beach in Alaska. It was the largest **colony** of walruses ever counted.

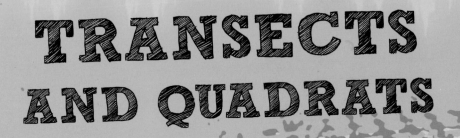

TRANSECTS AND QUADRATS

Most animals are smaller than the size of a thumbnail. They live in all kinds of places but do not move far. To count small bugs, scientists use two types of surveying technique.

FOLLOW THE LINE

Bugs live in every **habitat** – in forests, meadows, beaches and even on the seabed. The animals spread out over the area. It would take too long to count them all. Instead, scientists use a transect survey. A transect is a survey along a single line that runs through the habitat. Researchers follow the line, counting every animal they find along the way. The process creates a record of the wildlife in the area. It tells scientists which species are common in the area and which ones are less common.

A scientist in scuba gear follows a transect across the seabed. She records every animal she sees - including this coral.

A researcher is collecting every creature he can find inside a quadrat. The big square is divided up into 100 smaller ones. This helps to record where every animal is found.

SQUARE SURVEY

A quadrat is a square frame that scientists place on the ground. Every insect, spider and other creature found in the quadrat is collected in a jar. Back in the **lab**, the animals are identified and counted. Scientists usually make several quadrat surveys of a habitat and combine the results. The surveys show how many different species live in the area. They are also used to estimate the populations of each species.

JOIN IN

Beach transect

A rocky beach is a great place to do your own transect. The tide washes over the beach each day. Animals at the top of the beach live in the air most of the time. Those living at the bottom are covered by water most of the time. Visit the beach at low tide, and walk slowly down to the water, while looking in the rock pools. Do the animals you see change as you get nearer to the water?

Beach wildlife forms zones. Each **zone** is filled with plants and animals that can survive in that zone of the beach.

COUNTING MOUNTAIN GORILLAS

The mountain gorilla is the world's most **endangered** species of **ape**. There are only 780 of them living in the wild. Scientists count the apes' nests to keep track of the population.

A group of tourists visits the gorillas. The money they pay is used to help protect these rare animals.

KEEPING CLEAR

All mountain gorillas live in the forests of East Africa. For years, people destroyed the forests and hunted the gorillas. Now the gorillas are protected by armed rangers. The rangers keep out of the gorillas' way. Too many human visitors makes the apes distressed and prevents them from behaving normally.

POPULATION COUNT

Gorillas live in groups called troops. Each troop lives in a patch of forest called its home range. The troops move around this area each day eating leaves. At dusk the adult gorillas build nests. They bend the branches of shrubs and small trees to make a comfortable sleeping area.

Researchers visit the troops from time to time to learn about their behaviour. Scientists also regularly count nests to keep track of the number of gorillas in each troop. If a troop's number goes down, rangers will investigate. A gorilla may have moved to another troop, or hunters may have been in the area.

A young gorilla rests in his nest. Gorillas build a new nest every day.

This map shows where the troops of gorillas live in Rwanda. Each troop is shown as a different colour. There are about 20 gorillas in each troop.

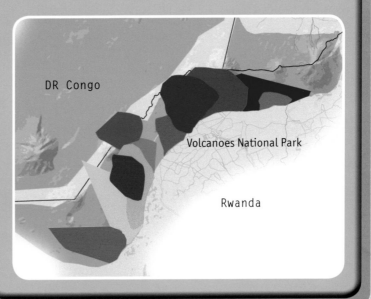

RWANDA: Gorilla troops

DR Congo

Volcanoes National Park

Rwanda

Africa

counting whales

Hunting whales is no longer allowed. Scientists want to know if the number of whales is increasing. To do this they need to count them carefully.

Whales were hunted by people for hundreds of years. They were killed for their meat and for the oil in their bodies. Whale hunting was banned in 1982. Scientists want to know if the number of whales has increased since the ban.

Hard to count

It is not easy for scientists to count whales. They use binoculars and telescopes to count them from the shore or from boats. But this method can only be an estimate. Whales spend most of their time far away from the shore in the deep oceans. Scientists can't see most of them. Researchers tried flying over the sea in planes, searching for whales to count. They found some whales this way, but a few of the planes crashed. A safer way of counting had to be found.

Southern right whale

Hunters killed southern right whales for many years. They were said to be the "right" whales to hunt because they were slow swimmers and easy to catch. People are no longer allowed to hunt them.

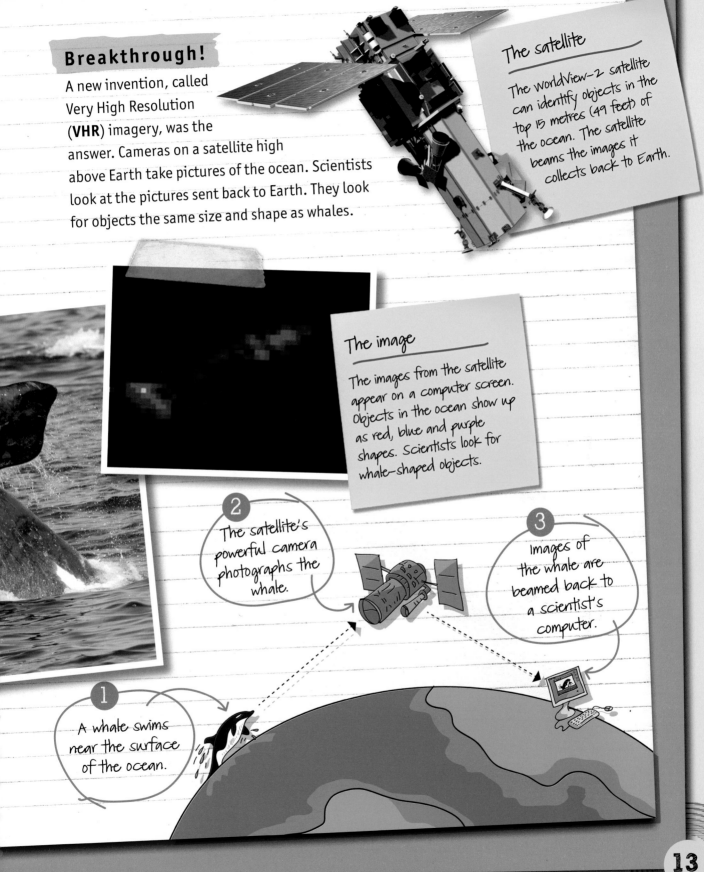

Breakthrough!

A new invention, called Very High Resolution (**VHR**) imagery, was the answer. Cameras on a satellite high above Earth take pictures of the ocean. Scientists look at the pictures sent back to Earth. They look for objects the same size and shape as whales.

The satellite

The WorldView-2 satellite can identify objects in the top 15 metres (49 feet) of the ocean. The satellite beams the images it collects back to Earth.

The image

The images from the satellite appear on a computer screen. Objects in the ocean show up as red, blue and purple shapes. Scientists look for whale-shaped objects.

1 A whale swims near the surface of the ocean.

2 The satellite's powerful camera photographs the whale.

3 Images of the whale are beamed back to a scientist's computer.

13

COUNTING BY SOUND

Nocturnal animals are difficult to see in the dark. This makes them hard to count. Scientists figure out how many animals there might be from the sounds they make.

MAKING NOISE

During the day the sounds of human activities drown out the calls of wildlife. In the quiet of night, it is easier to hear these sounds. Because **vision** is not so useful in the dark, many animals rely on their sense of hearing. They also communicate with sounds.

A scientist records the sounds of bats flying overhead. Individual bats make different sounds, so scientists can figure out how many bats there are.

Owls are difficult to see during the day. The best way to count them is to listen for their night-time calls.

JOIN IN

Counting owls

Did you know that the tawny owl sound "twit twoo" is made by two birds? One is calling and the other is replying. Search for this organisation online and check out their collection of recorded owl calls:

Wild Owl Educational Services

Listen to the way owls call to each other. Can you identify the owls that live near you? How many are there?

SOUND SURVEY

Animals use sounds to defend a **territory**. Sounds are also signals that warn about danger. Most importantly, animals call to attract mates. For all these calls to work, they must be particular to each species. Wildlife experts can identify the animals in an area from the sound of their calls. This helps scientists count their numbers.

RECORDING EQUIPMENT

The human ear cannot pick up many animal calls. Special equipment is used instead. Tiny variations in a roar or other call can identify one individual from another. Human hearing cannot tell them apart, but computers can analyse recordings of calls and show how many different animals are making them.

A wolf howls to let other wolves know it is there. Other wolves howl back.

RECORDING FROG CALLS

Automatic sound recorders are used to help count frog populations. The information they collect shows scientists where frogs gather in large numbers.

SOUND SAMPLES

The technique used for counting animal sounds is called Passive **Acoustic** Sampling. Automatic recorders, or data loggers, are set up in different habitats. They do not record everything all the time. Instead, they record a short period of sound at regular intervals. These sounds may be loud or soft.

IN THE SWAMP

Data loggers were used to carry out frog surveys in the Okefenokee Swamp in Georgia, in the southern United States.

This male green tree frog calls to mates from the treetops. The female lays eggs on leaves that float on water. When the eggs hatch, the tadpoles fall into the water.

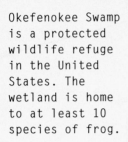

Okefenokee Swamp is a protected wildlife refuge in the United States. The wetland is home to at least 10 species of frog.

The swamp has several different habitats, including wetland forest, flooded prairie, and dry woodland. Researchers used data loggers to record frog calls in all of these habitats throughout the year. The scientists listened to the recordings and identified each frog species by its call. They also added up how many times they heard that species in each recording.

RESULTS

The acoustic sampling programme showed that most frogs lived in the prairie. The most common species was the southern cricket frog. Its calls were heard in three-quarters of recordings. By contrast, the green tree frog was less common. Only three out of every 100 recordings detected one of its calls.

TECHNOLOGY: Data logger

The data logger recorded one minute of sound every hour. It was programmed to turn on at night. This is when the frogs make most of their calls.

FACT: Poisonous frogs call louder than other frogs. They don't need to worry about attracting predators.

Songbird territories

When it is time to breed, a male songbird starts to sing. Counting the number of songs is a good way to estimate the total songbird population.

Songbirds, such as warblers, breed in summer when there is plenty of food around. The females and their nests are hidden in trees, but the males are much easier to spot.

Finding males

During the summer breeding season, male songbirds develop bright colours to attract a mate. The male and female pair will work together all summer, building a nest and feeding their chicks. To attract a mate, male songbirds set up a territory in a tree or bush. This is where he and his mate will build the nest. The male attracts females to his territory by singing. He does this mostly in the morning and evening. (He feeds in the middle of the day.) As well as signalling to females, the song warns other males to stay out of his territory.

Recorder

This sound recorder can pick up bird songs that are too quiet for human ears to hear. Its wide dish collects the faint sounds and focuses them onto the microphone in the middle.

Nest estimate

Scientists count the songs of each species. This tells them how many breeding territories there are. Most males find a mate. Doubling the number of territories gives the area's total bird population.

Migrations

Many songbirds, such as warblers, **migrate** to cooler areas to breed. Population surveys are important because they show how many birds are making the journey.

American warbler

This insect-eating songbird species, the bay-breasted warbler, migrates from South America to New England and eastern Canada each year. The male (left) sets up a mating territory in the forest.

2 For every calling male there is also a female in a nest.

1 A researcher records the bird songs in the forest.

3 The scientist follows a transect through the forest while making recordings.

19

COUNTING
WITH TRAPS

Animal trappers used to be people who caught animals for food or for their fur. Modern scientists also trap animals so they can count them. When possible, the animals are released unhurt.

WHAT'S OUT THERE?

Traps are used to find animals that live alone most of the time, such as raccoons. Traps are also good at capturing animals, such as wolves, that travel long distances and are hard to track.

A diver watches as a lobster is lured into a basket trap. The lobster will climb in to eat the food inside. It won't be able to climb out again.

The lantern bug is just one of many insect species that lives in rainforest trees.

WOW!

Scientists in rainforests have an unusual way of counting the insects in a tree. They spray the tree with an insecticide, a chemical that kills all the insects. Scientists use a machine to shake the trunk. All the dead insects fall down onto a sheet spread on the ground. One tree can contain around 1,500 species of insects.

Traps are also used in places that are hard for humans to get to. For example, scientists use traps to survey octopus and lobster populations on the seafloor.

CATCH AND RELEASE

Scientists cannot trap every animal. They use a special method to figure out how many there might be. Every trapped animal is marked with an identity tag. This is often attached to a ring on the leg or clamped to the ear. Researchers will count how many times these tagged animals are caught in other traps. If tagged animals are re-trapped many times, that tells researchers that there may not be many members of that species in the area. If new, untagged animals regularly appear in the traps, that shows there is a large population.

TRAPPING MAMMALS

Scientists use traps to study many types of mammals, from bears to badgers. The type of trap they use depends on how big the animal will be and how it will behave.

USING BAIT

Most mammal traps are baited. That means an animal is lured to the trap by a supply of its favourite foods. When the animal touches the bait, the trap is triggered. Small mammals are trapped in boxes or cages. The animal needs to go right inside to reach the bait. When it is inside, a door swings shut behind it.

A researcher prepares to examine a large bat trapped in a net. He must be careful or the bat will bite him.

TAKING CARE

Mammals are not harmed by these traps. Scientists check the traps every day and let the animals go free. Small mammals, like voles or squirrels, will starve to death if they are left inside for too long.

OTHER TRAPS

Bats are caught in nets strung up between trees. Bats cannot see the fine netting so they fly straight into it. Researchers remove the bats gently so their delicate wings don't get hurt. Larger mammals, such as wolves and bears, are captured in spring-powered leg-hold traps. When the animal walks on the trap, jaw-like grips grab its leg so it cannot run away. The grips are covered in rubber so they do not hurt the animal.

This raccoon is trapped in a live mammal trap. It can be tagged to see if it is the only one in the area.

TECHNOLOGY: Live mammal trap

There is only one way into the trap. The door is held open by a hook holding the bait.

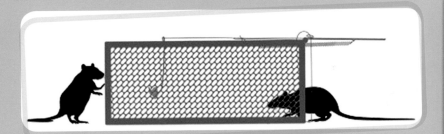

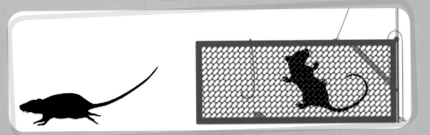

When the animal (such as a rat) grabs the bait, the door hook is released. The door swings shut.

MOTH
LIGHT TRAPS

Moths and other insects that fly at night are attracted to lights. Scientists make use of this behaviour to make simple traps.

A light trap in a tropical forest will attract many moths and other insects.

GUIDED BY LIGHT

No one is quite sure why moths are attracted to light. One theory is that moths use light to guide them as they fly through the night. The brightest natural light comes from the Moon. Moths might fly towards it so they know they are always going in the same direction. An **artificial** light is even brighter than the Moon. It confuses the moths' sense of direction.

LIGHT TRAPS

Scientists trap moths by hanging a white sheet in a forest and shining a bright light onto it. The moths fly towards the light and land on the sheet. Scientists collect interesting species in jars. They count all the species that land on the sheet. There will be several members of a common species but only one or two rarer ones.

Other light traps are boxes or drums with a see-through plastic lid. A light inside shines out through the lid. Moths are attracted to the light and crawl through gaps in the lid. Ripped-up paper or soft cardboard is put inside the trap. The moths climb in among the warm shreds and stay there.

Trapping shows that big moths, such as this emperor moth, are widespread. However, only a few of these moths live in each area.

FACT: A male emperor moth can smell a female from 8 kilometres (5 miles) away.

Salamander traps

Pitfall traps are used to capture salamanders and newts. These simple traps are easy to make.

Salamanders and newts have four legs and a long tail. They are **amphibians** related to frogs. Unlike many frogs, salamanders spend a lot of time out of water. They can be trapped with a simple plastic tub buried in the soil.

Pitfall trap

A salamander trap is a type of pitfall trap. This is a pit that an animal falls into and cannot get out of. Pitfall traps are used to trap beetles, spiders and centipedes. They are used to trap any small crawling animal. Salamanders live in damp places, such as forests. Scientists set up traps in these places to see what species are there. A few salamanders climb into the trap – and cannot escape. Trapping surveys like this show which species are most common in the area.

Pitfall trap

The simplest pitfall trap is a plastic tub buried in the ground. Salamanders, such as a fire salamander (below), like to hide in dark places, so it is also a good idea to cover the tub with a flat stone or piece of wood.

A researcher examines a giant salamander that has travelled onto land.

Using a trap

The trap must contain damp soil so the animal does not dry out. Check the trap every few hours. Hold any salamander you catch by the body, not by the tail. It will break off.

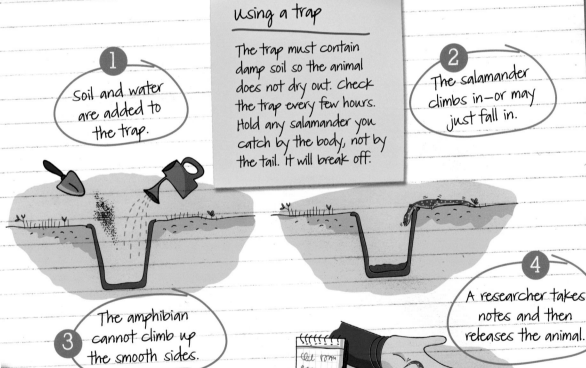

1 Soil and water are added to the trap.

2 The salamander climbs in—or may just fall in.

3 The amphibian cannot climb up the smooth sides.

4 A researcher takes notes and then releases the animal.

THE FUTURE

By counting and tracking animals, scientists know that many species are disappearing. In the future new techniques will be used to track them. This will help scientists protect endangered animals.

Remote-controlled drones send back live video of wild animals. They can be used to track herds of elephants and check their numbers.

TAKING TO THE AIR

Scientists can keep track of animals in remote places by using uncrewed aircraft, or drones. A drone can fly over a wide area more quickly than people can travel on the ground. Drones are already used to keep watch over endangered animals.

Locusts swarm when the population gets very large. They set off in search of a new home.

A locust swarm flying over Albuquerque, New Mexico, is picked up by a weather radar. The cloud of insects is 1.5 kilometres (5,000 feet) thick.

PATTERN RECOGNITION

In the future images and videos taken by drones overhead could be used to count all kinds of animals in a habitat. Computers are good at recognising patterns. They are already used for identifying human faces and fingerprints. The same kind of pattern-recognition system could one day identify the distinctive body shapes and fur patterns of many animals in the pictures from the drone. The computer could then count all the animals automatically.

SATELLITE SCANS

Individual animals are too small to show up in **satellite** images. However, large flocks of birds and insect swarms can be seen with the **radar** used in weather satellites. Scientists are still figuring out what different groups of animals look like on radar scans. The thickness of the flock seen by radar could be used to estimate how many animals it contains.

GLOSSARY

acoustic to do with sound

amphibians animals that spend their lives in water as well as on land

ape type of mammal, like a monkey but without a tail

artificial not natural

colony group of animals that gathers to live in a particular place

endangered in danger of becoming extinct

estimate guess made using a scientific technique

extinct no longer existing

habitat place where animals or plants live and grow

lab short for "laboratory," a workspace where a scientist works

migrate regular journey made by animals as they move to new locations to find food, to find mates, and to raise young

nocturnal active at night and at rest during the day

radar technology that bounces radio waves off objects and picks up any echoes that come back. The system is used to detect large objects that are too far away to see with the naked eye.

satellite object that orbits (moves around) another larger object. Planets are satellites of the Sun; moons are satellites of a planet. Machines launched into orbit are also known as satellites.

solitary alone

species group of animals that can breed with each other

superpod several pods that have gathered together. A "pod" is the name for a group of dolphins or whales.

survey examination using a scientific technique. The results of a survey can be compared with those of other surveys.

territory in terms of biology, a region controlled by an animal. The animal finds all its food in the territory and tries to stop other members of its species from living there.

Very High Resolution (VHR) system that takes detailed pictures of Earth's surface from space

vision sense of sight

zone area

READ MORE

Big RSPB Birdwatch: Get to know the birds outside your window. David Chandler. London: Bloomsbury, 2011.

Mammals (Classifying Animals). Sarah Wilkes. London: Wayland, 2007.

RSPB Guide to Nature Watching. Mark Boyd. London: Bloomsbury, 2013.

Spot 50 Butterflies and Moths: How to Identify 50 species. Camilla de la Bedoyere. Thaxted, UK: Miles Kelly, 2011.

INTERNET SITES

Wild Owl Educational Services
How to find out if owls live in your area.
www.wildowl.co.uk

Big Garden Bird Watch
Information on an annual garden bird survey.
www.rspb.org.uk/birdwatch

National Owl Pellet Survey
Ways to estimate mammal numbers by looking at the contents of owl pellets.
www.mammal.org.uk/owl_pellet_survey

Bat Kids
Information on bats that live in the UK.
www.bats.org.uk/pages/batsforkids.html

Buglife
How to work out the number of insects living in an area.
www.buglife.org.uk/tags/kids

INDEX